W9-CDE-652

The What Color Is Your
Parachute
Workbook

How to Create a Picture of
Your Ideal Job or Next Career

by
Richard N. Bolles

Ten Speed Press
Berkeley, California

Robertson

Introduction

IN ORDER TO HUNT FOR ANY JOB, it is important to have a picture of Your Ideal Job clearly in your head. That way, if you have to choose something less than your Ideal Job, you'll know where to compromise, and where not to.

We have chosen a "Flower" as a model for that picture of Your Ideal Job. This, because like a Flower, you will flourish in some (work) environments, and not in others. Where you flourish, you will do your best, most effective and happiest work.

Our "Flower" has eight petals, and we work our way through them starting with the quickest petals to fill out, and then working our way gradually to the eighth, which is the longest one.[1] This is what your "Flower" will look like at the end, except it will be larger, and in color, and all filled out[2]:

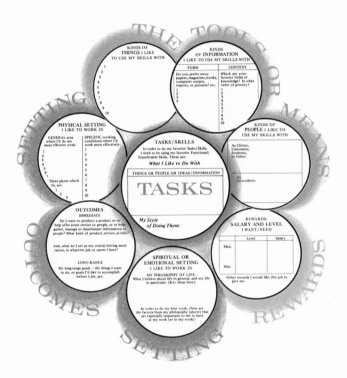

The order in which you will work on the eight petals is:

1. My Favorite Kinds of Things That I Like to Work With
2. My Favorite Kinds of Information That I Like to Work With
3. My Favorite People to Work With
4. My Favorite Rewards at Work
5. My Favorite Spiritual or Emotional Setting
6. My Favorite Outcomes, Immediate and Long-range
7. My Favorite Physical Setting
8. My Favorite Transferable Skills

Okay? So, get out your pen or pencil, and let's get started.

---

1. If this booklet is being used in a workshop, the leader may prefer to work on the eighth petal *throughout* the time you are working on the other ones, doing one new *story* at each session.
2. A large poster of the Flower ("The Anatomy of a Job") is available, suitable for writing on, for $4.95 each plus $2 postage and handling for the first one, and 50 cents for each additional. California residents please add local sales tax. Send check or money order to Ten Speed Press, P.O. Box 7123, Berkeley, CA 94707.

Step One:
My Favorite Kinds Of Things That I Like To Work With

Almost any kind of job involves some work with Things. For example, if you are a farmer, you work with tractors, perhaps a storage silo, a barn, etc. If you are an airline agent, you work with computers, tickets, staple machines, etc.

If you hate working with the Things your job requires, you will end up hating that job. It is therefore useful for you to decide, even before you know what kind of job you would like, just what kinds of Things you would like to be around.

Following is a list of various kinds of Things. Check the box in front of any words that describe a Thing you enjoy being around. You don't have to say, yet, what you want to do with it. *Maybe* you just want it in the background at your job. *Maybe* you want to actually handle it, on the job. *Maybe* you want to help make it or produce it. You don't have to say, yet.

Check it off, if for any reason it's one of your favorite Things. Add any Thing left off the following list, that you enjoy.

Things I Enjoy Working With:

Types of Material
- ☐ Paper
- ☐ Pottery
- ☐ Pewter
- ☐ Paraffin
- ☐ Papier-mâché
- ☐ Wood
- ☐ Other crafts materials
- ☐ Bronze
- ☐ Brass
- ☐ Cast iron, ironworks
- ☐ Steel
- ☐ Aluminum
- ☐ Rubber
- ☐ Plywood
- ☐ Bricks
- ☐ Cement
- ☐ Concrete, cinder-blocks
- ☐ Plastics
- ☐ Textiles
- ☐ Cloth
- ☐ Felt
- ☐ Hides
- ☐ Synthetics
- ☐ Elastic
- ☐ Crops
- ☐ Plants
- ☐ Trees

Types of Manufactured Stuff
- ☐ Machines
- ☐ Tools
- ☐ Toys
- ☐ Equipment
- ☐ Controls, gauges
- ☐ Products

- ☐ **Financial Things**
  - ☐ Calculators
  - ☐ Adding machines
  - ☐ Cash registers
  - ☐ Financial records
  - ☐ Money

- ☐ **Office Related Things**
  - ☐ PBX switchboards
  - ☐ Desks, tables
  - ☐ Desktop supplies
  - ☐ Pens, ink, felt-tip, ballpoint
  - ☐ Pencils, black, red or other
  - ☐ Typewriter
  - ☐ Computers
  - ☐ Copying machines, mimeograph machines, printers

☐ **Housing Items**
- ☐ Tents
- ☐ Trailers
- ☐ Apartments
- ☐ Houses
  - ☐ Chimneys
  - ☐ Columns
  - ☐ Domes
  - ☐ Carpenter's tools
  - ☐ Paint
  - ☐ Wallpaper
  - ☐ Heating elements, furnaces
  - ☐ Carpeting
  - ☐ Fire extingishers, fire alarms, burglar alarms
  - ☐ Household items
    - ☐ Furniture
    - ☐ Beds
    - ☐ Sheets, blankets, electric blankets
    - ☐ Laundry
    - ☐ Washing machines, dryers
    - ☐ Washday products, bleach
    - ☐ Kitchen appliances, refrigerators, microwaves, ovens, dishwashers, compactors
    - ☐ Kitchen tools
    - ☐ Dishes
    - ☐ Pots and pans
    - ☐ Can openers
    - ☐ Bathtubs
    - ☐ Soaps
    - ☐ Cosmetics
    - ☐ Toiletries
    - ☐ Drugs
    - ☐ Towels
    - ☐ Tools, power tools

☐ **Old Equipment**
- ☐ Clocks
- ☐ Telescopes
- ☐ Microscopes

☐ **Energy Things**
- ☐ Fuel cells
- ☐ Batteries
- ☐ Transformers, electric motors, dynamos
- ☐ Engines, gas, diesel
- ☐ Windmills
- ☐ Waterwheels
- ☐ Water turbines
- ☐ Gas turbines
- ☐ Steam turbines
- ☐ Steam engines
- ☐ Dynamite
- ☐ Nuclear reactors

☐ **Foods or Food Manufacturing Equipment**
- ☐ Wells, cisterns
- ☐ Meats
- ☐ Breads and other baked goods
- ☐ Health foods
- ☐ Vitamins
- ☐ Dairy equipment
- ☐ Winemaking equipment

☐ **Clothing Items**
- ☐ Clothing
- ☐ Raingear, umbrellas
- ☐ Spinning wheels, looms
- ☐ Sewing machines
- ☐ Patterns, safety pins, buttons, zippers
- ☐ Dyes
- ☐ Shoes

☐ **Electrical and Electronics**
- ☐ Radios
- ☐ Records
- ☐ Phonographs
- ☐ Stereos
- ☐ Tape recorders
- ☐ Cameras
- ☐ Television cameras
- ☐ Television sets
- ☐ Videotape recorders
- ☐ Movie cameras, film
- ☐ Electronic devices
- ☐ Electronic games
- ☐ Lie detectors
- ☐ Radar equipment

☐ **Amusement, Recreation**
- ☐ Games
- ☐ Cards
- ☐ Board games, checkers, chess, Monopoly, etc.
- ☐ Kites
- ☐ Gambling devices or machines

☐ **Musical Instruments**
- ☐ Specify:

☐ **Communication Things**
- ☐ Telephones, answering machines
- ☐ Cellular phones
- ☐ Telegraph
- ☐ Fax machines, teleprinters
- ☐ Voice mail machines
- ☐ Ship-to-shore radio, shortwave, walkie-talkies

☐ **Printing Materials**
- ☐ Printing presses, type, ink

☐ **Art Materials**
- ☐ Woodcuts, engravings, lithographs
- ☐ Paintings, drawings, silkscreens

☐ **Reading Materials**
- ☐ Books, braille books
- ☐ Newspapers
- ☐ Magazines

☐ **Educational Materials**
- ☐ Transparencies

☐ **Manufacturing or Warehouse Supplies**
- ☐ Dollies, handtrucks
- ☐ Containers
  - ☐ Bottles
  - ☐ Cans
  - ☐ Boxes
- ☐ Automatic machines
- ☐ Valves, switches, buttons
- ☐ Cranks, wheels, gears, levers
- ☐ Hoists, cranes

☐ **Things that Produce Light**
- ☐ Matches
- ☐ Candles
- ☐ Lanterns, oil lamps
- ☐ Light bulbs, fluorescent lights
- ☐ Laser beams

☐ **Gym Equipment**

☐ **Sports Equipment**
- ☐ Fishing rods, fishhooks, bait
- ☐ Traps, guns

Prioritizing Your List

□ **Gardening or Farm Equipment**
- □ Garden tools
- □ Shovels
- □ Picks
- □ Rakes
- □ Lawnmowers
- □ Ploughs
- □ Threshing machines, reapers, harvesters
- □ Fertilizers
- □ Pesticides
- □ Weed killers

□ **Transportation Things**
- □ Land
  - □ Roads
  - □ Bicycles
  - □ Motorcycles
  - □ Mopeds
  - □ Automobiles
  - □ Parking meters
  - □ Traffic lights
  - □ Trains
  - □ Subways
- □ Air
  - □ Gliders
  - □ Balloons
  - □ Airplanes
  - □ Parachutes
- □ Sea
  - □ Rivers
  - □ Lakes
  - □ Streams
  - □ Canals
  - □ Ocean
  - □ Boats
  - □ Steamships
- □ Other vehicles

□ **Medical Materials or Equipment**
- □ Medicines
- □ Vaccines
- □ Anesthetics
- □ Thermometers
- □ Hearing aids
- □ Dental equipment
- □ X-ray machines
- □ False parts of the human body
- □ Spectacles, glasses, contact lenses

Good. Now you've got a list. You'll have several lists before you're through with this booklet.

But, lists will do you no good whatsoever--*unless* you know which item on the list is The Most Important to you, and which item is Next Most Important, and so forth. This is called *Prioritizing*. You *must* prioritize each list, beginning with the list you just checked off--your list of Favorite Things.

How do you go about doing that? Well, first of all, you circle what you would *guess* to be your top ten favorite things, from among all the boxes you checked. You can't decide which are your top ten? Then choose your top twenty-four. We've got a device to help you, either way.

If you chose ten Favorite Things, then use the Grid on page 6. If you chose your top twenty-four Favorite Things, then use the Grid on page 7.

● First step in using either Grid is:
write in the items you have chosen,
in no particular order,
in Section A, of the Grid.

● Second step, in using either Grid is:
you begin to compare
just two items at a time,
to each other,
as the small boxes indicate,
starting with the box in Section B
that says 1 2.
Let's take that box. Here's how you use it:
You say to yourself,
"IF I COULD HAVE JOB #1,
that lets me use the Thing
I wrote in space number 1,
but not the Thing
I wrote in space number 2;
OR
IF I COULD HAVE JOB #2,
that lets me use the Thing
I wrote in space number 2,
but not the Thing
I wrote in space number 1,
WHICH JOB WOULD I TAKE?
(No fair, saying "Neither")
Make a choice, even if it's by *a hair.*
You then circle,
in the little box that has a 1 and a 2 in it,
whichever Thing
you decided was more important
to you, at a Job.
Then you go on,
comparing all the other Things,
two by two,
as the numbers in the little boxes indicate,
asking the same *kind* of question.

Prioritizing Grid for 10 Items

Each time you use this grid, make a photocopy of it, and fill in the photocopy rather than the original. (You will need to photocopy this grid many times as you go through this map. If you don't want to do that, and you have a personal computer that is an IBM or IBM-compatible, there is a computer program on a 5.25-inch disk that prints this Grid for you. You can order it, for a $5 check made out to Ron Grossman, 9 Union Sq., Suite 212, Southbury, CT 06488.)

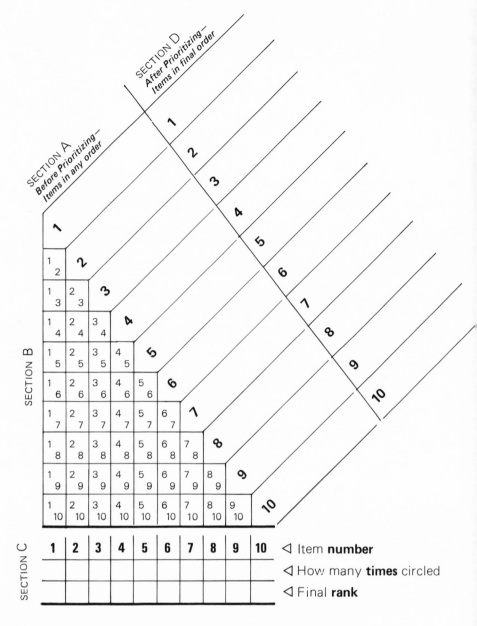

										◁ Item **number**
1	2	3	4	5	6	7	8	9	10	
										◁ How many **times** circled
										◁ Final **rank**

SECTION C

Copyright © 1989 by Richard N. Bolles. All rights reserved.

When you are done with all the boxes in Section B, you count up the number of circled numbers. First you count how many times you circled number 1, in *all* the little boxes in Section B. You then write that total down, on line #2 of Section C, under the figure 1. Go on with all the other numbers, filling in line 2.

Then you count which number got the most circles on line two, and you give the ranking of #1 to it, on the *third* line of Section C. Write in a figure 1, right below the highest number on line 2. Write in a figure 2, right below the next highest number on line 2. And so forth, and so on, until you have the rankings.

[If you have a tie, that is, if two items are circled the same number of times, you look back in Section B to see--when those two were compared there--which of the two you *preferred*. And you give *that item* an extra half point, thus breaking the tie.]

Now, it's time to fill in Section D. Look back at the bottom line of Section C. Let us say that item #7 *in Section A,* turned out to get the largest number of circles, and so ended up as **rank** #1. In *Section D,* now, on line number one, you copy that item. Or whatever item, *in your case,* turned out to have rank #1.

Likewise, on line 2 *in Section D,* you copy down your item that ended up in rank #2. And so forth, and so on.

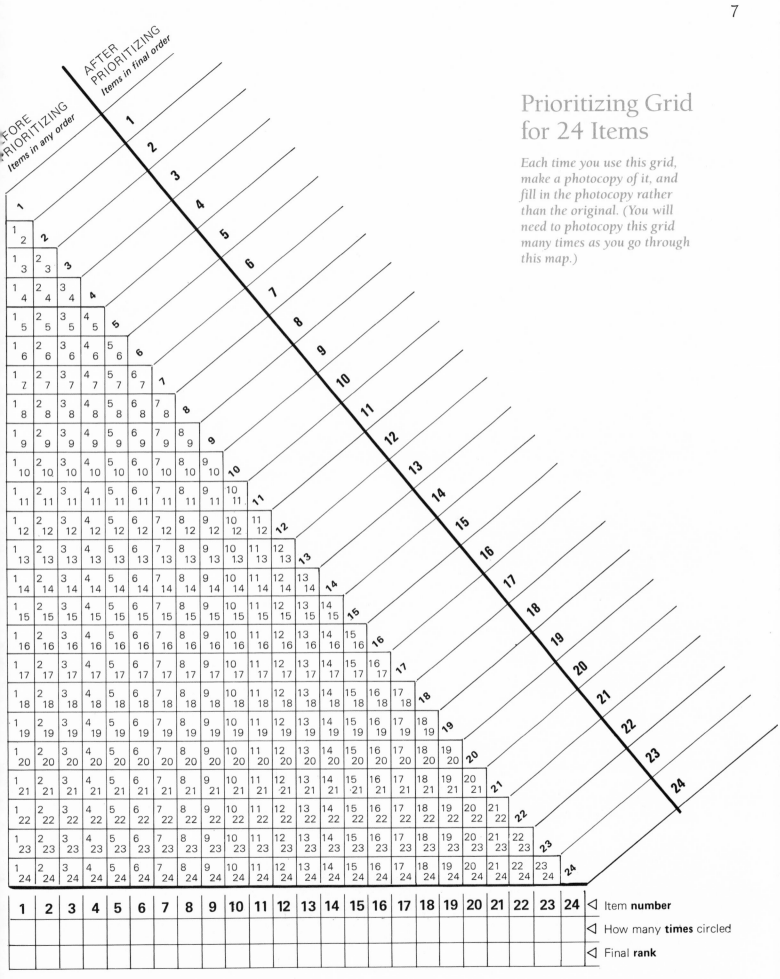

Prioritizing Grid for 24 Items

Each time you use this grid, make a photocopy of it, and fill in the photocopy rather than the original. (You will need to photocopy this grid many times as you go through this map.)

	Item **number**
	How many **times** circled
	Final **rank**

Copyright © 1989 by Richard N. Bolles. All rights reserved.

Now, regardless of which grid you used, copy your top ten Favorite Things here:

THE FIRST PETAL

My Favorite Kinds of Things

Kinds of
THINGS *I Like To*
Use My Skills With

1.

2.

3.

4.

5.

6.

7.

8.

9.

10.

Step Two:
My Favorite Kinds Of Information That I Like To Work With

Now we go on to the next petal. This one asks you what kinds of Information or Ideas or Fields you like to work with. As you will see on the petal on page 12, you want to ask yourself what *forms* of information you prefer to read or work with, as well as what *content*.

Form is a matter of: Do you prefer to work with information in the form of newspapers, magazines, books, computer output, reports, pictures, or what?

Following is a more complete list of such forms. Put a checkmark in front of any word (or phrase) below that describes forms of information you enjoy (or think you would enjoy) working with at your place of work. Add any others that occur to you, which are not on this list. Then when you are done checking, pick the seven that you think are **most** important to you, and copy them onto the left hand side of the petal on page 12. Do use the Prioritizing Grid (10 or 24 items), *first,* please, just as you did with Your Favorite Things.

Forms of Information I Prefer to Work with, or Help Produce:

- ☐ Books
- ☐ Magazines
- ☐ Newspapers
- ☐ Catalogs
- ☐ Handbooks
- ☐ Records, files
- ☐ Trade or professional literature
- ☐ Videotapes
- ☐ Audiotapes
- ☐ Computer printouts
- ☐ Seminars, learning from trainers
- ☐ Courses, learning from teachers
- ☐ Words
- ☐ Number or statistics
- ☐ Specifications
- ☐ Precision requirements
- ☐ Statistical analyses
- ☐ Data analysis studies
- ☐ Financial needs

- ☐ Costs
- ☐ Accountings
- ☐ Symbols
- ☐ Designs
- ☐ Blueprints
- ☐ Wall-charts
- ☐ Time-charts
- ☐ Schema
- ☐ Facts
- ☐ History
- ☐ Ideas
- ☐ Conceptions
- ☐ Investigations
- ☐ Opinion-collection
- ☐ Points of view
- ☐ Surveys
- ☐ Research projects, research and development projects, project reports
- ☐ Procedures
- ☐ Guidebooks
- ☐ Manuals

I Like to Collect or Deal with Information about Any of the Following:

- ☐ Principles
- ☐ Physical principles
- ☐ Spiritual principles
- ☐ Values
- ☐ Standards
- ☐ Repeating requirements
- ☐ Variables
- ☐ Frameworks
- ☐ Organizational contexts
- ☐ Boundary conditions
- ☐ Parameters
- ☐ Systems

- ☐ Programs
- ☐ Operations
- ☐ Sequences
- ☐ Methods
- ☐ Techniques
- ☐ Procedures
- ☐ Specialized procedures
- ☐ Analyses
- ☐ Data analysis studies
- ☐ Schematic analyses
- ☐ Intuitions

I Like to Help Put Information to Use in Any of the Following Practical Ways:

- ☐ Principles applications
- ☐ Recommendations
- ☐ Policy recommendations
- ☐ Goals
- ☐ Project goals
- ☐ Objectives
- ☐ Solutions
- ☐ New approaches

- ☐ Plans
- ☐ Tactical needs
- ☐ Performance characteristics
- ☐ Proficiencies
- ☐ Deficiencies
- ☐ Reporting systems
- ☐ Controls systems

If this checklist doesn't seem relevant to your life, don't worry about it. It helps some people *(a lot),* while it leaves others cold. Anyway, one way or another, when you are done with this checklist, and have listed your top seven on the left hand side of the petal on page 12, then it is time to turn from Form to **Content.** Content is on the right hand side of that same petal.

Content is a matter of: Among the fields that you know something about, which ones are your favorites? Do you love the knowledge you have about computers, or the knowledge you have about cars, or the knowledge you have about the Environment, or your knowledge of antiques, or gardening, or skiing, or painting, or psychology, or the Bible--or what?

A field is always *a subject,* or a *major* (as in college), or *"Principles of...,"* or *"How to...,"* or *"Rules of...,"* or *"The Secrets of...,"* etc.

Generally speaking, you picked up such knowledges in four different ways (at least), and these four ways form a handy chart for recalling to yourself what are the fields you know something about. *(See next page)*

Fields of Knowledge That You Learned About

In School or College (At Home or Work)	On the Job, or Just by Doing (At Home or Work)	From Seminars or Workshops	By Personal Instruction from People or by Reading a Lot

You want to list **all** the fields you know anything about, this first time 'round, whether you **like** them or not. You can go back later and check off your favorites, as well as cross out the ones you just hate.

Here are some *examples* to guide you in filling in the chart:

Fields of Knowledge I Learned About in School or College

e.g., *Spanish*   *Accounting*
Psychology   *Music appreciation*
Biology   *Typing*
Geometry   *Sociology*

Fields of Knowledge I Learned About on the Job, or Just by Doing (at Home or Work)

e.g., *How to operate a computer*
  How a volunteer organization works
    Principles of planning and management

Fields of Knowledge I Learned from Seminars or Workshops

e.g., *The way the brain works*
Principles of art
Speed reading
Drawing

Fields of Knowledge I Learned About by Personal Instruction from People or by Reading a Lot

e.g., *How to sew*
How to drive an automobile
How computers work
Principles of comparison shopping
Knowledge of antiques
Principles of outdoor survival

You may want to see a list, or at least a sampler, of other possible fields of knowledge, just to jog your memory. Following is such a list. Put a check mark in front of any word (or phrase) that describes possible fields of knowledge that you already are familiar with, and would enjoy getting a chance to use in your ideal job. Write in any others that occur to you, as you go down this list.

A SAMPLER OF POSSIBLE FIELDS YOU MAY KNOW ABOUT

Primarily about People

- ☐ Sociology
- ☐ The *how to* of customer relations and service
- ☐ Principles of group dynamics
- ☐ Principles of behavioral modification
- ☐ Instructional principles and techniques
- ☐ Organization planning
- ☐ Manpower requirements analysis and planning
- ☐ Personnel administration
- ☐ Recruiting
- ☐ Performance specifications

Primarily about Things

- ☐ Physics
- ☐ Astronomy
- ☐ Chemistry
- ☐ Computer programming
- ☐ Knowledge of a particular computer and its applications
- ☐ Design engineering
- ☐ Interior decorating
- ☐ How to run a particular machine
- ☐ Horticulture
- ☐ Car repairs
- ☐ Industrial applications
- ☐ Government contracts
- ☐ Maintenance
- ☐ Financial planning and management
- ☐ Bookkeeping
- ☐ Fiscal analysis, controls, reductions and programming
- ☐ Accounting
- ☐ Taxes
- ☐ R & D program and project management
- ☐ Merchandising
- ☐ Systems analysis
- ☐ Packaging
- ☐ Distribution
- ☐ Marketing/sales

Other Fields (not easily categorized)

- ☐ Principles of art
- ☐ Cinema
- ☐ Principles of recording
- ☐ Knowledge of foreign countries (which ones?)
- ☐ Musical knowledge and taste
- ☐ Graphic arts
- ☐ Photography
- ☐ Broadcasting
- ☐ How to make videos
- ☐ Linguistics or languages
- ☐ Spanish
- ☐ Music
- ☐ Policy development
- ☐ Religion

You will *of course* want to know if you can put down some field that you are **not** yet knowledgeable about, but think you would just *love* to learn about and use in your future ideal job. Well, sure, if you are absolutely, one hundred per cent, planning on studying that field in the near future. Or if you want to find a volunteer job or an apprenticeship where you could pick up knowledge of that field *on the job*. But let's not *just* talk about what you do not yet have; in addition to these, **do** list knowledges *you already possess*, as well. (*In other words, don't duck the exercise.*)

When you are all done listing or checking off all the fields you already know something about, *then* go back over the list and check your favorites, as well as cross out the ones you just hate. And, from among your favorites, pick the ten that you feel are **most** important to you to be able to use in your future ideal job, (from both the chart *and* this list). Then use the Prioritizing Grid to put those Top Ten Favorite Knowledges (or Top Twenty-Four) into exact order. Copy the Top Ten onto the petal on the next page.

Step Three: My Favorite People to Work With

Every job involves *some* work with People, whether as clients/customers/pupils/patients/listeners, or as co-workers. If the people are those toward whom your work is directed, the question is: *what kinds of people?* For example, suppose that you love to teach. The question now is: What people do you most enjoy teaching? All people? Particular age groups? If so, *which ones?* People with particular problems? If so, *which ones?* People who are working on particular issues in their life? If so, *which ones?*

On page 13 you will find a varied list of different kinds of people. Check those whom you particularly like (or think you would particularly like) to work with--as clients, customers, students, or whatever, in your work. Add any others that may occur to you, which are not on the list. Then when you are done checking, pick the ten that you think are **most** important, and use the Prioritizing Grid to prioritize those ten. Then list these on the petal on page 14.

My Favorite
Kinds of Information

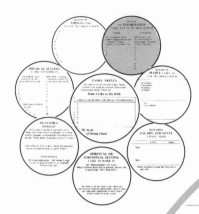

Kinds of
INFORMATION *I Like To*
Use My Skills With

FORM	CONTENT
e.g., "Do you prefer to work with information in the form of newspapers, magazines, books, computer output, reports, or pictures?" etc.	Among the fields of knowledge which you know something about, which ones are your favorites? And in what order of priority?
1.	1.
2.	2.
3.	3.
4.	4.
5.	5.
6.	6.
7.	7.
	8.
	9.
	10.

My Preferred Co-workers:

I prefer to work with what kinds of co-workers or colleagues, bosses, or subordinates?

- ☐ Both sexes
- ☐ Men primarily
- ☐ Women primarily
- ☐ People of all ages
- ☐ Adolescents or young people
- ☐ College students
- ☐ Young adults
- ☐ People in their thirties
- ☐ The middle-aged
- ☐ The elderly
- ☐ The retired
- ☐ All people regardless of sexual orientation
- ☐ Heterosexuals
- ☐ Homosexuals
- ☐ All people regardless of background
- ☐ People of a particular background
- ☐ People of a particular cultural background
- ☐ People of a particular economic background
- ☐ People of a particular social background
- ☐ People of a particular educational background
- ☐ People of a particular philosophy or religious belief
- ☐ Certain kinds of workers (blue-collar, white-collar, executives, or whatever)
- ☐ People in a particular place (the Armed Forces, prison, etc.)
- ☐ People who are easy to work with
- ☐ People who are difficult to work with

Kinds of People I Prefer to Serve, Or Try to Help:

- ☐ Men
- ☐ Women
- ☐ Individuals
- ☐ Groups of eight or less
- ☐ Groups larger than eight
- ☐ Babies
- ☐ School-age children
- ☐ Adolescents or young people
- ☐ College students
- ☐ Young adults
- ☐ People in their thirties
- ☐ The middle-aged
- ☐ The elderly
- ☐ The retired
- ☐ All people regardless of age
- ☐ Heterosexuals
- ☐ Homosexuals
- ☐ All people regardless of sex
- ☐ People of a particular cultural background

- ☐ People of a particular economic background
- ☐ People of a particular social background
- ☐ People of a particular educational background
- ☐ People of a particular philosophy or religious belief
- ☐ Certain kinds of workers (blue-collar, white-collar, executives, or whatever)
- ☐ People who are poor
- ☐ People who are powerless
- ☐ People who wield power
- ☐ People who are rich
- ☐ People who are easy to work with
- ☐ People who are difficult to work with
- ☐ People in a particular place (the Armed Forces, prison, etc.)

Kinds of Problems I Like to Try to Help People With:

- ☐ Physical handicaps
- ☐ Overweight
- ☐ Mental retardation
- ☐ Pain
- ☐ Disease in general
- ☐ Hypertension
- ☐ Allergies
- ☐ Self-healing, psychic healing
- ☐ Terminal illness
- ☐ Holistic health
- ☐ Life/work planning or adjustment
- ☐ Identifying and finding meaningful work
- ☐ Job-hunting, career change, unemployment, being fired or laid off
- ☐ Illiteracy, educational needs
- ☐ Industry in-house training
- ☐ Performance problems, appraisal
- ☐ Low energy
- ☐ Nutritional problems
- ☐ Physical fitness
- ☐ Work satisfaction
- ☐ Discipline problems, self-discipline
- ☐ Stress
- ☐ Sleep disorders
- ☐ Relationships
- ☐ Personal insight, therapy
- ☐ Loneliness
- ☐ Boredom
- ☐ Complaints, grievances
- ☐ Anger
- ☐ Anxiety
- ☐ Fear

- ☐ Shyness
- ☐ Meeting people, starting friendships
- ☐ Communications, thoughts, feelings
- ☐ Love
- ☐ Self-acceptance and acceptance of others
- ☐ Learning how to love
- ☐ Marriage
- ☐ Competing needs
- ☐ Sexual education, sexual problems
- ☐ Sexual dysfunction
- ☐ Pregnancy and childbirth
- ☐ Parenting
- ☐ Physical abuse
- ☐ Rape
- ☐ Divorce
- ☐ Death and grief
- ☐ Addictions
- ☐ Drug problems
- ☐ Alcoholism
- ☐ Smoking
- ☐ Mental illness
- ☐ Depression
- ☐ Psychiatric hospitalization
- ☐ Personal economics
- ☐ Financial planning
- ☐ Possessions
- ☐ Budgeting
- ☐ Debt bankruptcy
- ☐ Values
- ☐ Ethics
- ☐ Philosophy or religion
- ☐ Worship
- ☐ Stewardship
- ☐ Life after death
- ☐ Psychic phenomena

When you are done with these lists, guess what your top ten favorite Clients, Customers or Students, might be (or your top twenty-four), and use the appropriate Prioritizing Grid to get them in exact order. Put the top *three or four* in the top half of the petal on the next page. Then do the same for your Co-workers list.

Why not *ten,* as on the two earlier petals? Because we found out *that* isn't as helpful as three or four. That's why.

My Favorite People

Kinds of PEOPLE. I Like To Use My Skills With

As Clients,
Customers,
Students, or
Other:

As Co-workers:

Step Four:
My Favorite Rewards at Work

Virtually all of us hope for some reward from our work. We want enough salary to put bread on the table, clothes on our back, a roof over our head, and enough left over to do some of the things we want to do with our life.

Beyond *that* reward, however, we want others. The *level* at which we work is one of them. For example, in your ideal job would you want to work:

☐ by yourself and for yourself;

☐ by yourself but for another person or organization;

☐ in *tandem* with one other person;

☐ as a member of a team of equals;

☐ as a member of a hierarchy where you carry out directions;

☐ as a member of a hierarchy where you are the boss or supervisor or owner;

☐ or what?

Jot down, on the petal, as many ideas or hunches as occur to you at the moment. You can always change them later (as indeed, you can change *any* petal) after you have conducted your own research or informational interviewing about your *flower* picture.

The petal, on the next page, also asks you to think out what is the *minimum* salary you would need from your next job or career, and what is the *maximum* salary you would like to have if things were ideal.

The minimum is particularly important, because in this day and age you have to know *before you walk in for a potential hiring-interview anywhere* just what is the figure below which you will starve to death. What does it take for you to *just get by*? That's what *minimum* is. It means: I would just barely have enough for my basic necessities, if my salary were this figure. Of course it's going to take some calculating, first. You're going to have to add up what your basic housing costs are, what your minimum food costs would be, and how much else you would *have* to have, just to get by.

You do this calculating *now,* and not when you're sitting in a hiring interview, they offer you a salary, and you don't know whether to take it or not. Of course you can always beg off, at that time, and say you need a night to think about it. But if the salary they offer is below your *minimum* it would be helpful to know *that* right on the spot. Hence the importance of this petal, and that question.

The maximum, of course, is your daydreams. Not what it would take for you to be *rich,* but what kind of salary you would love to be able to earn so as to live *very comfortably.* In other words, to calculate your maximum, you put in *generous* amounts for each of your necessities and your optional activities. Add them all up, and you have your maximum.

At the bottom of this petal, you will see that space has been provided for you to add any other rewards that you would like your ideal job to give you. What do we mean by this? Well, many people hope their job will give them more by way of reward, than just money. *For example* (put a check mark in front of any that apply to you):

☐ Social contact   ☐ Respect
☐ A chance to help others   ☐ Adventure
☐ A chance to bring others closer   ☐ Challenge
   to God   ☐ Influence
☐ Intellectual stimulation   ☐ Security
☐ A chance to use my expertise   ☐ Independence
☐ A chance to make decisions   ☐ Wealth
☐ A chance to be creative   ☐ Power
☐ A chance to exercise leadership   ☐ Fame
☐ A chance to be popular

Grab a photocopy of the Prioritizing Grid for ten items, and put these in order. Then put them on the petal on the next page, please.

My Favorite Rewards

Salary and Level I Want/Need

	LEVEL	SALARY
MAX		
MIN		

Other rewards I would like this job to give me:

Step Five:
Spiritual or Emotional Setting

Your values affect strongly whether or not you will be happy at your job. Suppose, for example, you don't like lying or cheating. Obviously, you don't want to work in a place where you have to lie and cheat. Yet there are such places. A man once called me on the phone to ask what he should do about a crooked contract his firm had just executed. I asked him who drew it up. He said, "I did. My boss said: Do it, or lose your job."

You need to think out, as part of your Ideal Job, which values are important to you in life - - in the realm of things we cannot see: values, what you are willing to stand up for, and what you are not willing to stand up for, what you care about.

The most useful way to do this is to take a piece of blank paper (or two) and write out on it your *philosophy about life*: which typically might include some statement of why you think we are here on earth, what it is that you believe we are supposed to do while we are here, what you think is important in life and what is not important, and which values of our society you agree with, and which ones you disagree with. As a suggested framework only, you might want to choose from among these elements (you *don't* have to use them all):

- Behavior: how you think we should behave in this world
- Beliefs: what your strongest beliefs are
- Choice: what you think about its nature and importance
- Community: what ways we belong to each other, and what you think our responsibility is to each other
- Compassion: what you think is its importance, and how it should be manifested in our daily life
- Confusion or ambivalence: how much you think we need to learn to live with
- Death: what you think about it and what you think happens after it
- Events: what you think makes things happen, and how we explain this to ourselves
- Free will: what you think about the question of whether things are 'preordained to happen' or whether our free will causes them to happen
- God: see *Supreme Being*
- Heroes and heroines: who yours are
- Human: what you think makes someone truly 'human'

- Love: what you think is its nature and importance, along with all its related words: forgiveness, grace, etc.
- Principles: what ones you are willing to stand up for, which ones you base your life on
- Purpose: why you think we are here on earth, what you think is the purpose of your life
- Reality: what comments you have to make about the nature of reality
- Sacrifice: what in life you think is worth sacrificing for, and what kinds of sacrifice you would be willing to make
- Self: what you believe about the self, ego, selfishness, selflessness
- Stewardship: what you think we should do with God's gifts to use
- Supreme Being: if you have a concept of a Higher Power, or God, what you think this Supreme Being is like
- Values: what ones you hold most dear, sacred, and important

To help you in this latter area, you might want to examine your thoughts about the importance of *truth* (in what areas, particularly, does truth most matter to you?), the importance of *beauty* (what kinds of beauty do you like best?), *moral issues* (which ones are you most concerned about - - justice, feeding the hungry, helping the homeless, comforting AIDS sufferers, or what?), and the importance of *love*. Don't just *write;* take time also to *think!* Jot down the key ideas of your philosophy in the top part of the petal on the next page.

When you are done writing your philosophy of life, the bottom part of this petal asks you to lift out of that philosophy any factors which are especially important to you at your future place of work, or in your future work. For example, your philosophy of life might have reminded you: "I have to work in a place where I am never asked to do anything dishonest." Or: "I want to be among loving, supportive co-workers, and not among people who are always backbiting or gossiping about everyone." Whatever occurs to you, after studying your philosophy, put this stuff down, in the bottom part of that petal.

And, voila! The fifth petal is all finished.

My Favorite Spiritual or Emotional Setting

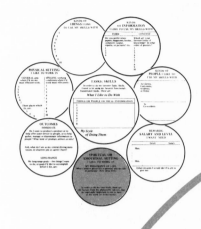

MY PHILOSOPHY OF LIFE.
What I believe about life in general,
and my life in particular
(key ideas here):

In order to do my best work,
these are the factors from my philosophy (above) that are especially important to me
to have at my work (or in my work):

Step Six:
My Favorite Outcomes, Immediate and Long-range

In the world of work, it is not enough merely to keep busy. One must be keeping busy for some purpose. We are talking about **outcomes,** or **where does it all lead to?** In the world of work, this is often called "the bottom line." I remember some years ago sending out two of my staff to find some materials for me, and after four hours' fruitless search, one turned to the other and said, "Well let's go back. At least we tried." And the other replied, "Unfortunately, in the world of work you're not usually rewarded for *trying;* you're only rewarded for *succeeding.*" So they kept on, until they found what they were looking for. This underlines the point here: generally speaking, when you set about to use your skills in the world of work, you must be aiming at some **result** --in accordance with some **purpose** or **goal,** defined by either you or the organization (preferably *both*).

So, look at the petal on page 21. There you will see that *Outcomes* divides into two parts: **Immediate** and **Long-range.**

Immediate Results of Your Work

Immediate results, at your place of work, is a matter of: "At the work I'd most love to do, what result am I aiming at? Do I want to help produce a **product,** or do I want to help offer some **service** to people, or do I want to help gather, manage, or disseminate **information** to people? Or all three? Or two? And in what order of priority? Do I think the world basically needs me to help it have: more information, or more service, or more of some product--such as food, clothing, or shelter?

Once you've answered that, the next question *of course* is: **what** product, or service, or information?

Well, the *what* is relatively easy to answer (I said *relatively*). If your preferred outcome is some **product** that you'd like to help produce or market, you'll probably find it identified on your *Favorite Things* petal, on page 8. If your preferred outcome is some **service** to people, you'll probably find it identified on your *Favorite People* petal, on page 14. And if your preferred outcome is some kind of **information** that you'd like to help gather, manage, or disseminate, you'll probably find it identified on your *Favorite Information* petal, on page 12.

This should give you the data you need, in order to fill in the top part of the next petal. If it doesn't, then postpone filling out that part of the petal until you've finished your last (eighth) petal. For that exercise, you will be asked to write out seven stories. When you have them all, come back to this petal, and ask yourself, what

20

Outcomes:
The Central Motivation - - One Result

To be completed after you have finished the eighth and final petal.

*Go through your seven stories and underline in purple all your verbs. See which of the verbs below get repeated over and over again. These describe **the one result** that you are always attempting to reach, **the one outcome** that you find to be your chief and most coveted reward, in all you do. You, of course, don't want to be pinned down to just one; you want to be able to choose three, or four, or more. Fine, just prioritize them afterward on a prioritizing grid.*

Acquire / Possess (*Money / Things / Status / People*) Wants to have own…baby, toys, possessions, houses, family. Chief reward: "This is mine."

Be in Charge / Command (*of Others / Things / Organization*) Wants to be on top, in authority, in the saddle - - where it can be determined how things will be done…Chief reward: "I decide."

Combat / Prevail (*over Adversaries / Evil / Opposing Philosophies*) Wants to come against the bad guys, entrenched status quo, old technology…Chief reward: "I won."

Develop / Build (*Structures / Technical Things*) Wants to make something where there was nothing…Chief reward: "I created this."

Excel / Be the Best (*versus: Others / Conventional Standards*) Wants to be the fastest, first, longest, earliest, or more complicated, better than others…Chief reward: 'I stood out."

Exploit / Achieve Potential (*of Situations / Markets / Things People*) Sees a silk purse, a giant talent, a hot product, or a promising market before the fact…Chief reward: "I had a vision of what it could be, and helped that vision to come true."

Gain Response / Influence Behavior (*from People / Through People*) Wants dogs, cats, people, and groups to react to their touch…Chief reward: "I got a warm response."

Gain Recognition / Attention (*from Peers / Public Authority*) Wants to wave at the cheering crowd, appear in the newspaper, be known, dance in the spotlight…Chief reward: "People know who I am."

Improve / Make Better (*Oneself / Others / Work / Organizations*) Makes what is marginal, good; what is good, better; what makes a little money, make a lot of money…Chief reward: "I made it better."

Make the Team / Grade (*Established by Others or the System*) Gains access to the varsity, Eagle Scout rank, Silver Circle, Thirty-ninth Masonic Order, the country club, executive dining room…Chief reward: "I did it!"

Meet Needs / Fulfill Expectations (*that are Demanded / Needed / or Inherent*) Strives to meet specifications, shipping schedules, what the customer wants, what the boss has expressed…Chief reward: "They're impressed with me."

Make Work / Make Effective (*Things / Systems / Operations*) Fixes what is broken, changes what is out-of-date, redesigns what has been poorly conceived…Chief reward: "Now it works."

Master / Perfect (*Some Subject / Skill / Equipment / Objects*) Goes after rough edges, complete domination of a technique, total control over the variables…Chief reward: "I mastered that."

Organize / Operate (*Business / Team / Product Line*) The entrepreneur, the beginner of new businesses…Chief reward: "I brought it into being."

Overcome / Persevere (*Obstacles / Handicaps / Unknown Odds*) Goes after hungry tigers with a popgun, concave mountains with slippery boots…Chief reward: "And they said it couldn't be done."

Pioneer / Explore (*Technology / Cultures / Ideas*) Presses through established lines, knowledge, boundaries…Chief reward: "To boldly go where no one has gone before."

Serve / Help (*People / Organizations / Causes*) Carries the soup, ministers to the wounded, helps those in need…Chief reward: "To make this world a kinder place."

Shape / Influence (*Material / Policy / People*) Wants to leave a mark, to cause change, to impact…Chief reward: "They won't forget me."

*(Adapted by Richard N. Bolles from Miller, Arthur F., and Mattson, Ralph T., **The Truth About You: Discover What You Should Be Doing With Your Life**, 1st ed., 1977, pp. 68-69. Not to be reproduced without written permission from Arthur Miller, People Management Inc., P.O. Box 33608, Seattle, WA 98133.)*

---

kind of outcomes did I usually strive for in my seven stories? Read them over again, to be sure. It is very likely you will find it all boils down to one of the motivations listed in Arthur Miller's chart (above). Or two. Or three. Put it on the petal.

The Long-range Results of Your Work

As a result of **all** the work you do here on earth, what results or outcome do you want to achieve by the time that you die? What goals do you want to accomplish, what things do you want to do? Your answer to this should be written out, thoughtfully, on a single piece of scratch paper (*no more than one page, please*) - - and then the most important points in your statement should be copied onto the bottom part of petal #6 on the next page. Go back, also, and look at your philosophy of life, on page 18.

Incidentally, if while you are writing this statement, you find yourself setting down some long-range goals that really have nothing to do with *your work* as such, but have to do more with your overall *life* - - such as, "Before I die, I want to travel all over the world" - - write them down *anyway*. You just never know when a job might be offered to you somewhere down the road that would make it possible for you to achieve some of your **life**-goals, and not just your work or achievement-goals.

THE SIXTH PETAL

My Favorite Outcomes

Immediate

At the work I'd most love to do,
do I want to help produce a **product**
or do I want to help offer some **service** to people,
or do I want to help gather, manage or disseminate **information** to
people? Or all three? Or two? And what kind of product, service, or info?

And, what do I see as my central driving motivation in whatever job I take, or in whatever career I pursue?

Long-range

My long-range goals for my life -- the things I want to do, or the goals
I'd like to accomplish -- before I die, are:

Step Seven: Physical Setting

Physical Setting means two things: in what part of the country do you want to live and work? And, at what kind of a place (physically) do you want to work there? We call these two factors *"Geography"* and *"Working Conditions."*

Geography may seem a silly thing to be worrying about in this day and age. You may be rooted to a particular place because you have a house you can't afford to sell, or your ailing parents are nearby. Nonetheless, it is useful to wrestle with this question, anyway. You never know when an opportunity may suddenly open up, for you, to move to your own idea of paradise. That is, *if* you know the name of that paradise.

Maybe it springs to your lips, even now. Whoops, not so fast. You need to know not only *its* name, but also the name of other places *like it.* That means you have to know the *factors* which make a particular place so attractive to you. Hence, the chart to the right. It's to help you remember all the places you have ever lived --and what factors you did or didn't like (mostly *didn't*) about that place.

The first column is self-explanatory.

The second column requires you to look at each name that is in the first column, and write down all the things you disliked, and still dislike, about that place. Write *small.* You'll need lots of room. Incidentally, you don't have to write the factors opposite the name of the place. Put them *anywhere* in column 2.

While doing this, you may think of some things you actually *liked* about a particular place. Put the *positives* in column 3, down near the bottom, as indicated. The purpose of the top part of column 3 is to look at what you've written in column 2, and turn all those *negatives* into *positive* form. For example, if one of the things you listed in column 2 was "too rainy most of the year," the positive form of that--for you to put in column 3-- would be "sunny most of the year." And so forth.

For column 4, you get out a photocopy of your Prioritizing Grid (probably the 24-Item one) and put your top twenty-four items in column 3 onto that grid, and prioritize them. The resulting top fifteen get listed in column 4.

To fill out column 5, you call your friends over for a friendly evening. You show them all the factors *in order* that you listed in column 4. And you ask them to suggest different places in the country (or the world, if you're willing to move far) that have the factors you listed-- or at least the *top* factors you listed. Don't stumble over

Decision Makin

Column 1 Names of Places I Have Lived	Column 2 From the Past: Negatives
	Factors I Disliked and Still Dislike about That Place

My/Our Geographical Preferences

or Just You			Decision Making for You and a Partner		
Column 3 slating the Nega- es into Positives	Column 4 Ranking of My Positives	Column 5 Places Which Fit These Criteria	Column 6 Ranking of His/Her Preferences	Column 7 Combining Our Two Lists (Columns 4 & 6)	Column 8 Places Which Fit These Criteria
	1.		a.	a. 1.	
	2.		b.	b. 2.	
	3.		c.	c. 3.	
	4.		d.	d. 4.	
	5.		e.	e. 5.	
	6.		f.	f. 6.	
	7.		g.	g. 7.	
	8.		h.	h. 8.	
	9.		i.	i. 9.	
	10.		j.	j. 10.	
ctors I Liked and Still Like about That Place	11.		k.	k. 11.	
	12.		l.	l. 12.	
	13.		m.	m. 13.	
	14.		n.	n. 14.	
	15.		o.	o. 15.	

two factors that seem to be contradictory, like "sunny and warm all year round" and "skiing nearby." There's *almost always* an answer. In this case, it's "Palm Springs, with the tram up Mt. San Jacinto there, to the skiing."

When your friends are through suggesting places, pick the one you like best, next best, and third best, and put them on the bottom left side petal #7 on the opposite page. If you don't know enough about them, put your three favorites in any order, and write away to their chambers of commerce, to find out more about them. The library also can help!

The last three columns are only to be used if you have a wife, husband, or partner, and you are doing joint decision-making about where you eventually want to move to. In that case, your partner will need to photocopy the Geography chart (before you fill it out, obviously) and do their own first five columns. If your preferred geographical areas turn out to be identical, then you are done with the chart. But if they don't, then go on to column #6 and copy your partner's positive factors from his or her column #4.

Now, on to column #7. Merge together, there, your "Ranking of My Positives" and your partner's ranking. Your factors, obviously, are numbered 1, 2, 3, 4, 5, etc. while your partner's are numbered a, b, c, d, e, etc. You will notice that column #7 asks you first to list your partner's top priority, then your top one, then your partner's second priority, then your second one, etc.

When done, move on to column #8. It involves exactly the same procedure as column #5. Show column #7 to all your friends and ask them what cities or towns they think of, when they read this (combined) list of factors. Again, don't be put off by apparently contradictory factors. There's usually some place, somewhere, that can give you both factors.

Time, now, to transfer all this to the left side of the petal on the opposite page. List your top seven factors from column 4 (or the top seven factors on you and your partner's *combined* list in column 7). And then list the top three places which you and your friends found fit these factors.

Working Conditions

Now that you have filled out the General Geographical half of the Physical Settings petal, on to the other half: Working Conditions.

You use the same method as you did for Geography. In fact you can make up a chart where you copy the first four columns (only) of the Geography Chart. The only change you will need to make is to relabel column #1 as "Names of Places I Have Worked." Here name all the companies, or all the jobs you have ever held.

Column #2, now, is "Factors I Disliked and Still Dislike About That Job." Examples would be "no windows," "a boss that oversupervised me," "had to come in too early," etc.

Columns #3 and #4 remain the same. List, and then prioritize, the positive factors about the working conditions you like best. Remember, these are also the working conditions under which you can do your best and most effective work. When you're done, list them on the right hand side of the petal on the opposite page.

My Favorite Physical Setting

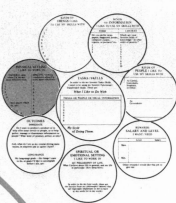

GENERAL
Geographical Factors

The geographical area which would please me most, and therefore help me to do my most effective work, would have the following factors (e.g., warm dry summers, skiing in the winter, a good newspaper, etc.):

1.

2.

3.

4.

5.

6.

7.

The names of three places which fit these factors are:

1.

2.

3.

SPECIFIC
Working Conditions

At my place of work I could be happiest and do my most effective work, if I had the following working conditions (e.g., working indoors or out, not punching a timeclock, a boss who gave me free rein to do my work, having my own office, etc.):

1.

2.

3.

4.

5.

6.

7.

8.

9.

10.

Step Eight: My Favorite Transferable Skills

Well, we've come to the eighth and final petal. We've also come to the one where you are going to do the most work, and the most thinking. This is the most important petal, for it is at *the heart* of *any* picture of An Ideal Job.

There are two ways for you to go, here. *Quick and dirty!* Or, *Slow and thorough.* Let's look at *Quick and dirty!* first. We use a device called:

The Party Exercise:
What Skills You Have and
Most Enjoy Using

As John L. Holland has taught us all, skills may be thought of as dividing into six clusters or families. To see which ones you are *attracted to,* try this exercise:

On the next page is an aerial view of a room in which a two-day (!) party is taking place. At this party, people with the same or similar interests have (for some reason) all gathered in the same corner of the room.

(1) Which corner of the room would you instinctively be drawn to, as the group of people you would most *enjoy* being with for the longest time? (Leave aside any question of shyness, or whether you would have to talk with them.) Write the *letter* for that corner here:

(2) After fifteen minutes, everyone in the corner you have chosen leaves for another party crosstown, except you. Of the groups *that still remain,* which corner or group would you be drawn to the most, as the people you would most *enjoy* being with for the longest time? Write the letter for that corner here:

(3) After fifteen minutes, this group too leaves for another party, except you. Of the corners, and groups, which remain now, which one would you most enjoy being with for the longest time? Write the letter for that corner here:

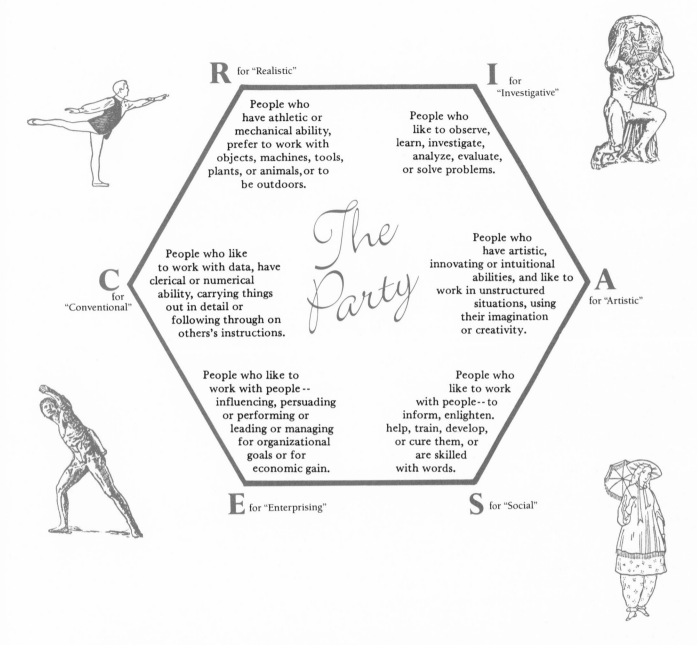

R for "Realistic"

I for "Investigative"

People who have athletic or mechanical ability, prefer to work with objects, machines, tools, plants, or animals, or to be outdoors.

People who like to observe, learn, investigate, analyze, evaluate, or solve problems.

The Party

People who like to work with data, have clerical or numerical ability, carrying things out in detail or following through on others's instructions.

People who have artistic, innovating or intuitional abilities, and like to work in unstructured situations, using their imagination or creativity.

C for "Conventional"

A for "Artistic"

People who like to work with people -- influencing, persuading or performing or leading or managing for organizational goals or for economic gain.

People who like to work with people -- to inform, enlighten. help, train, develop, or cure them, or are skilled with words.

E for "Enterprising"

S for "Social"

(If you simply shudder at the thought of filling out the rest of the pages in this booklet, and you want instead to stay with this Holland theory of careers, you are advised to take the following steps: (1) Order a Self-Directed Search Specimen Set from Psychological Assessment Resources, Inc., Box 998, Odessa, FL 33556. When you receive it, do the Self-Directed Search booklet. It will take you about an hour's time. (2) When you are done with it, you will have a three-letter "Holland Code" for yourself (for example, SIA). Then look up that code in the Dictionary of Holland Occupational Codes: A Comprehensive Cross-Index of Holland's RIASEC Codes with 12,000 DOT Occupations -- which your library should have; if it does not, you will have to order the book from Psychological Assessment Resources (above). When you have the book in front of you, see what occupations are suggested for your code (e.g., SIA). (3) Also look up the occupations for the other arrangements of your code (e.g., SIA can also be arranged as SAI, or ISA, or IAS, or ASI, or AIS). Look up suggested occupations for each of these combinations. (4) Then go to your library, find the DOT (Dictionary of Occupational Titles) there, and look up the occupations on your list from steps 2 and 3 above. Pick four or five occupations, from among this list, that seem particularly interesting to you, and notice what skills the DOT says such jobs require. (5) Ask yourself, and your friends, if you have those skills. If so, there is your skills list.)

Now, on to "Slow, but Absolutely Thorough."

In order to find out this information, it will be necessary for you to write out seven (7) stories of some enjoyable and satisfying experiences or accomplishments which you have done in your life. Which stories should you choose? Ah, that's a good question. Not necessarily the ones which occur to you right off the top of your head. Sometimes you have to dig deeper.

To guard yourself against impulsively choosing stories which may not tell you much about your skills, it is helpful to construct a basic outline of your life, for yourself, first. One way to do this is through a Memory Net.

The Memory Net

That Net is to the right. You should take at least three hours (with some hard thinking, as well as writing) to fill it in.

In the first column of the Memory Net are the years of your life, divided into five-year periods (cross out the years before your birth, of course). Some of you will be able to remember what activities you were doing during each of these five-year periods, just from seeing the dates. Use this column, then, to jog your memory, and fill in the rest of the Net.

The second column is for those of you who don't remember things by Dates, but by what job you were holding down, or what school you were attending, or organizations you were involved with, or people who were influential upon your life, etc. Use this column, then (with whatever title you want to put on it), to jog your memory--fill it in, and then fill in the rest of the Net.

The third column is for those of you who don't remember things by either Years or Jobs, but by where you were living at the time. Use this column, then, to jog your memory--fill it in, and then fill in the rest of the Net.

Once you've tackled the first three columns, as you go across the rest of the Memory Net you will generally find it pays to fill in the three Activities columns first (columns 4, 6, and 8), and then go back to the Accomplishments columns (5, 7, and 9). That is to say, once you remember what you were *doing* (activities) in the way of Leisure, Learning, or Labor (Work), you will then find it easier to think of specific accomplishments in your Leisure or your Learning or your Labor. Put down titles only, or a few words to jog your memory, rather than attempting any more detailed description of your accomplishments, at this time.

Jogging Your Memory

Column 1 In Terms of Five-Year Periods	*Column 2* In Terms of Jobs You Have Held	*Column 3* In Terms of Places You Have Lived
e.g. 1988-1992		
1983-1987		
1978-1982		
1973-1977		
1968-1972		
1963-1967		
1958-1962		
1953-1957		
1948-1952		
1943-1947		
1938-1942		
1933-1937		

Memory Net

Leisure		Learning		Labor	
Column 4	*Column 5*	*Column 6*	*Column 7*	*Column 8*	*Column 9*
Activities	Accomplishments	Activities	Accomplishments	Activities	Accomplishments

Once you have the Net all filled out, you are ready to choose and write your stories. See the form on the opposite page, called *Life Story No. _____*? You will need to make 7 photocopies of this, since you will need to write seven stories. If you think each story will take more than one page, then make 14 photocopies of the page opposite.

For the time being, you start by writing **just one** of those stories. Look over your Memory Net, and most particularly at columns 5, 7, and 9. Look at your accomplishments. Whether they were early in your life, or more recently, whether they were in your leisure life, or your learning life, or your labor/work life, does not matter.

Just be sure also that it deals in turn with TASK, TOOLS or MEANS, and OUTCOME or RESULT. See the example that follows:

---

1. A TASK. Something you wanted to do, just because it was fun or would give you a sense of adventure or a sense of accomplishment. Normally there was a problem that you were trying to solve, or a challenge you were trying to overcome, or something you were trying to master or produce or create.

2. TOOLS or MEANS. You used something to help you do the task, solve the problem, overcome the challenge. Either you had certain *Things* to help you--objects, materials, tools or equipment, or you had other *People* to help you, or you got a hold of some vital *Information*. Tell us what tools or means you used, and how you used them.

3. AN OUTCOME or RESULT. You were able to finish the task or solve the problem, overcome the challenge, master a process, or produce or create something. You had a sense of pride, even if no one else knew what it was you had accomplished.

© *Copyright 1988 by D. Porot. Adapted and used by his permission.*

Once you have selected your first story, write it out in detail--but keep it comparatively brief--two or three paragraphs at most. Be sure that it is *a story* you tell --that is, that it moves step by step. It may help if you pretend that you are telling it to a small whining child who keeps saying, "An' then whadja do?" "An' then whadja do?"

When you are done, label that sheet "#1".

This won't do.
Too brief.

This will do.

Life Story No. ___

d then whadja do? And then whadja do? And then whadja do? And then whadja do? And then whadja do? And then whadja do?
d then whadja do? And then whadja do? And then whadja do? And then whadja do? And then whadja do? And then whadja do?

STORY

SKILLS USED in this life story of yours. In front of each skill put the number of the line in the life story where that skill was demonstrated.

STORY	SKILLS USED
1	
2	
3	
4	
5	
6	
7	
8	
9	
10	
11	
12	
13	
14	
15	
16	
17	
18	
19	
20	
21	
22	
23	
24	

d then whadja do? And then whadja do? And then whadja do? And then whadja do? And then whadja do? And then whadja do?
d then whadja do? And then whadja do? And then whadja do? And then whadja do? And then whadja do? And then whadja do?
d then whadja do? And then whadja do? And then whadja do? And then whadja do? And then whadja do? And then whadja do?

Identifying Your Skills

Once this first story is written, you are ready to identify what skills you used, in that story. The list of skills you are to use is found on the next three pages. The skills resemble a series of typewriter keys. You go down each column vertically. As you look at each key, you ask yourself, "Did I use this skill **in this story?** (story #1)." If you did, you color in the little box *right under* that key which has the number 1 in it (color right *over* the "1"). We suggest you use a **red** pen, pencil, or crayon, to do this coloring in. Keep going down each column, in turn, on each of the following three pages.

When you are done with all the skills keys, for Things, People, and Information, you have finished with story #1. You now know what skills you used while you were doing this first enjoyable achievement, that you have selected to analyze.

However, "one swallow doth not a summer make," and the fact you used certain skills in this one accomplishment doesn't yet tell you much. What you want to look for are patterns: i.e., which skills keep getting used, again and again, in accomplishment after accomplishment, story after story. It is *the patterns* that are meaningful for choosing your future job or career.

So now it is time to take the second sheet of paper, label it "#2", and look over the Memory Net to see which achievement you want to pick for your second story. Once you have selected it, and written it out in detail, you go back to the Skills Keys and again ask yourself, "Did I use this skill **in this story?** (story #2)." And, again, if you did, you color in the little box right under that key that has the number 2 in it (color right over the "2"). Again, use the red pen, pencil, or crayon. Continue through the three skill pages.

Take the third sheet and repeat the process, and so, continue on through sheet (and story) #7. When you are done, look over the three Skill Pages to see which skills stand out (i.e., which ones have *the little boxes* under them colored in the most).

Choosing Your Favorites from Among All Your Transferable Skills

From those three pages, choose your ten favorite skills--the ones you do best, *and* enjoy the most. Never mind whether those skills were with Things, or People, or Information. It could turn out, for example, that eight of your favorite skills are with Things, and one with Information, and one with People. It doesn't matter. On a photocopy of the Prioritizing Grid, now (the ten-item one is best), list what you have concluded, by guess and by gosh, are your ten favorite skills. You want to use the grid so that you end up with a list of your top eight Favorite Skills *in order*--where the skill you most enjoy using is #1, the skill you next most enjoy using is #2, and so forth.

Optional: Restating Skills in Your Own Language

Now that you have a list of your favorite skills, *in order,* you *may* want to restate these in other language or other words. Maybe there are other skill words that you would feel more comfortable with. To help you with this task of *translation,* there is an Appendix at the back of this booklet, beginning on page 45. Turn there, look up each skill--it will be in bold type--and see if you prefer any of the words that are offered as alternatives there. You can, of course, rephrase any of those words into language that is *completely yours,* if you want to. Put your top eight favorite skills, in these new words, onto the petal on page 37.

Of course if you like the old words, stick with them, and copy *them* onto the petal on page 37. The point is to end up with your top eight favorite skills listed *in order* on that petal.

If you prefer a visual display, you may enter your top eight favorite skills also on the Building Block diagram, that you will find on page 38.

'Fleshing Them Out'

A *complete* identification of a transferable skill of yours *should* (in the end) have three parts to it: verb, object, and modifier (adjective or adverb). Now that you have *the verb* in your own language you *may* want to flesh out each of your favorite skills so that each one also has some general *object* and *modifier,* e.g., "organizing" fleshed out to "organizing ideas logically."

My transferable skills dealing with
THINGS

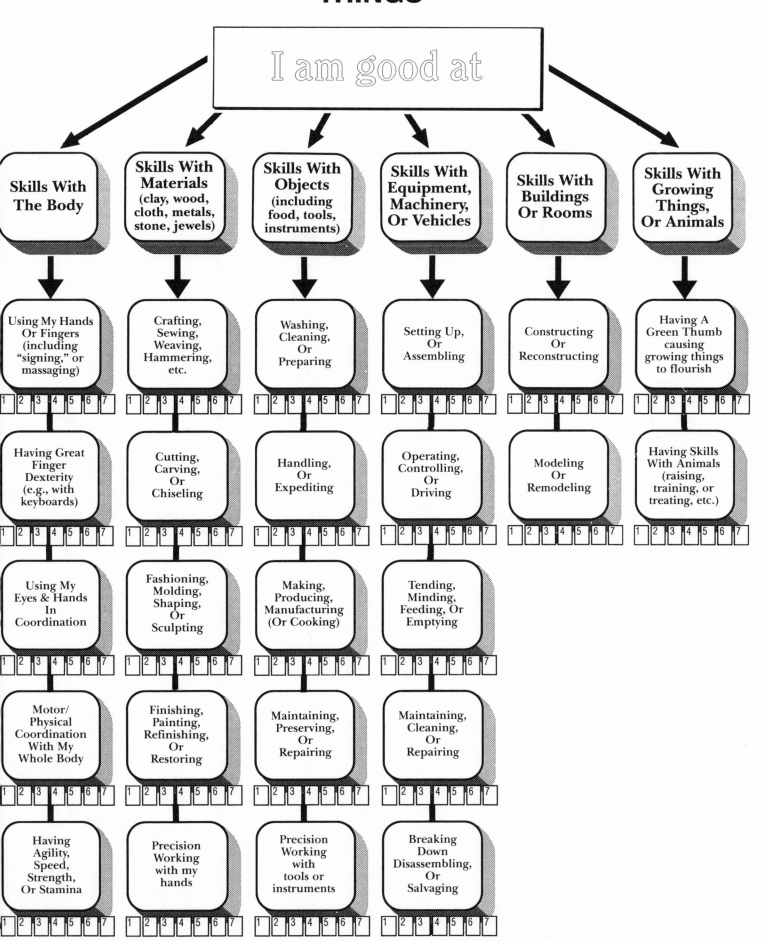

My transferable skills dealing with

PEOPLE

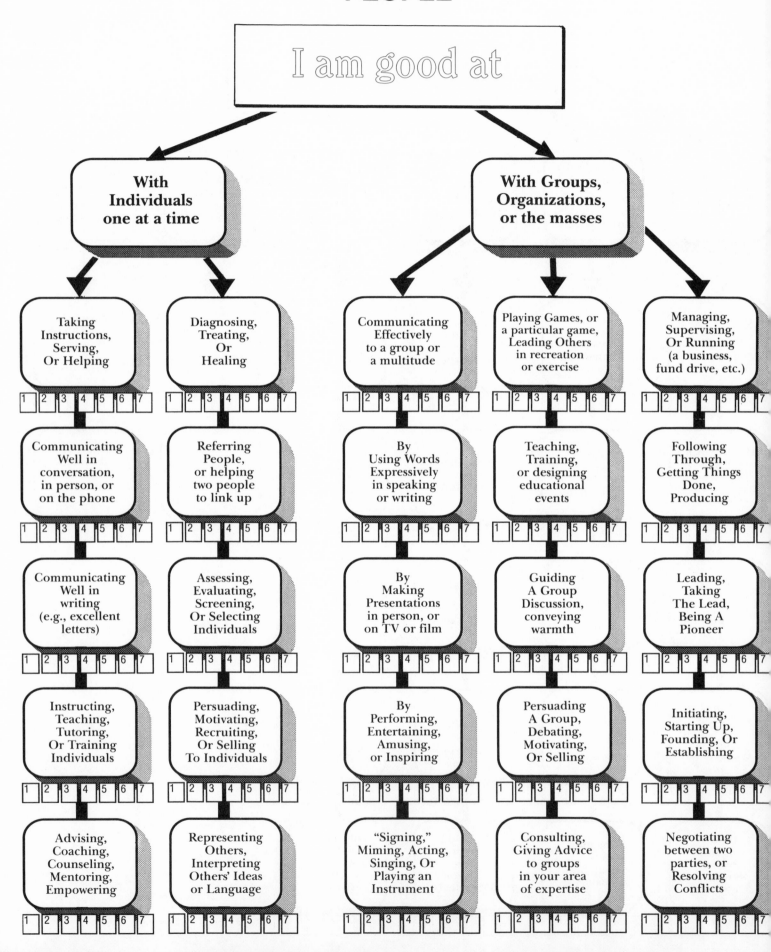

I am good at

With Individuals one at a time

With Groups, Organizations, or the masses

Taking Instructions, Serving, Or Helping	Diagnosing, Treating, Or Healing

1 2 3 4 5 6 7   1 2 3 4 5 6 7

Communicating Well in conversation, in person, or on the phone	Referring People, or helping two people to link up

1 2 3 4 5 6 7   1 2 3 4 5 6 7

Communicating Well in writing (e.g., excellent letters)	Assessing, Evaluating, Screening, Or Selecting Individuals

1 2 3 4 5 6 7   1 2 3 4 5 6 7

Instructing, Teaching, Tutoring, Or Training Individuals	Persuading, Motivating, Recruiting, Or Selling To Individuals

1 2 3 4 5 6 7   1 2 3 4 5 6 7

Advising, Coaching, Counseling, Mentoring, Empowering	Representing Others, Interpreting Others' Ideas or Language

1 2 3 4 5 6 7   1 2 3 4 5 6 7

Communicating Effectively to a group or a multitude	Playing Games, or a particular game, Leading Others in recreation or exercise	Managing, Supervising, Or Running (a business, fund drive, etc.)

1 2 3 4 5 6 7   1 2 3 4 5 6 7   1 2 3 4 5 6 7

By Using Words Expressively in speaking or writing	Teaching, Training, or designing educational events	Following Through, Getting Things Done, Producing

1 2 3 4 5 6 7   1 2 3 4 5 6 7   1 2 3 4 5 6 7

By Making Presentations in person, or on TV or film	Guiding A Group Discussion, conveying warmth	Leading, Taking The Lead, Being A Pioneer

1 2 3 4 5 6 7   1 2 3 4 5 6 7   1 2 3 4 5 6 7

By Performing, Entertaining, Amusing, or Inspiring	Persuading A Group, Debating, Motivating, Or Selling	Initiating, Starting Up, Founding, Or Establishing

1 2 3 4 5 6 7   1 2 3 4 5 6 7   1 2 3 4 5 6 7

"Signing," Miming, Acting, Singing, Or Playing an Instrument	Consulting, Giving Advice to groups in your area of expertise	Negotiating between two parties, or Resolving Conflicts

1 2 3 4 5 6 7   1 2 3 4 5 6 7   1 2 3 4 5 6 7

My transferable skills dealing with
INFORMATION, DATA, AND IDEAS

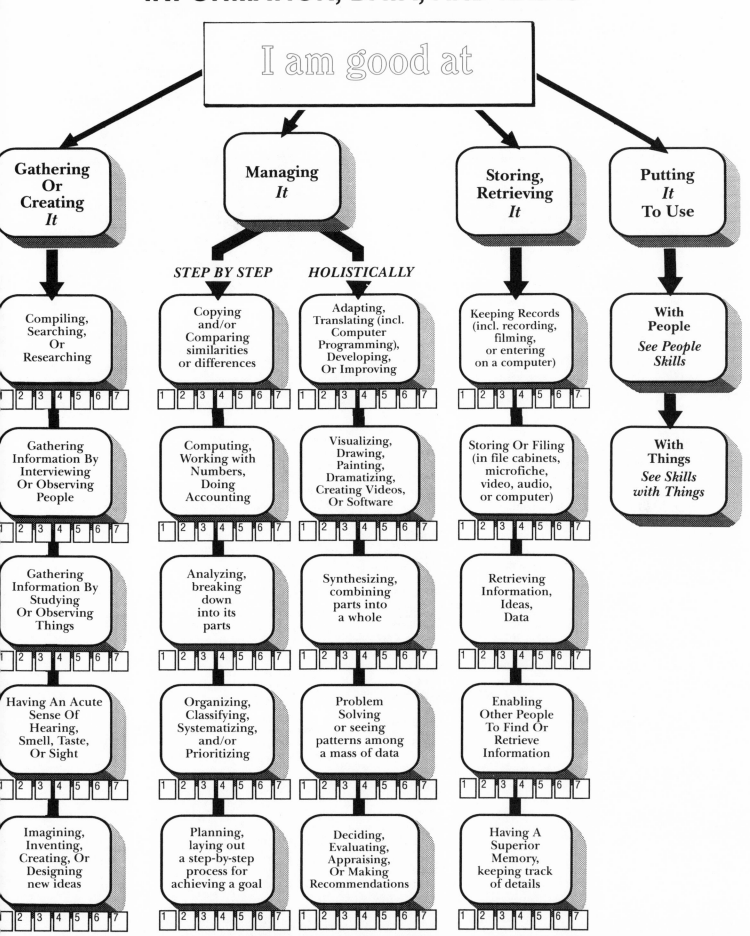

I am good at

Gathering Or Creating *It*

Managing *It*

STEP BY STEP

HOLISTICALLY

Storing, Retrieving *It*

Putting *It* **To Use**

Compiling, Searching, Or Researching

Copying and/or Comparing similarities or differences

Adapting, Translating (incl. Computer Programming), Developing, Or Improving

Keeping Records (incl. recording, filming, or entering on a computer)

With People *See People Skills*

2 3 4 5 6 7 · 1 2 3 4 5 6 7 · 1 2 3 4 5 6 7 · 1 2 3 4 5 6 7

Gathering Information By Interviewing Or Observing People

Computing, Working with Numbers, Doing Accounting

Visualizing, Drawing, Painting, Dramatizing, Creating Videos, Or Software

Storing Or Filing (in file cabinets, microfiche, video, audio, or computer)

With Things *See Skills with Things*

2 3 4 5 6 7 · 1 2 3 4 5 6 7 · 1 2 3 4 5 6 7 · 1 2 3 4 5 6 7

Gathering Information By Studying Or Observing Things

Analyzing, breaking down into its parts

Synthesizing, combining parts into a whole

Retrieving Information, Ideas, Data

2 3 4 5 6 7 · 1 2 3 4 5 6 7 · 1 2 3 4 5 6 7 · 1 2 3 4 5 6 7

Having An Acute Sense Of Hearing, Smell, Taste, Or Sight

Organizing, Classifying, Systematizing, and/or Prioritizing

Problem Solving or seeing patterns among a mass of data

Enabling Other People To Find Or Retrieve Information

2 3 4 5 6 7 · 1 2 3 4 5 6 7 · 1 2 3 4 5 6 7 · 1 2 3 4 5 6 7

Imagining, Inventing, Creating, Or Designing new ideas

Planning, laying out a step-by-step process for achieving a goal

Deciding, Evaluating, Appraising, Or Making Recommendations

Having A Superior Memory, keeping track of details

2 3 4 5 6 7 · 1 2 3 4 5 6 7 · 1 2 3 4 5 6 7 · 1 2 3 4 5 6 7

Your *Style* of Working

At the bottom of *The Tasks/Skills petal* on the opposite page, space is provided for you to list **the style** with which you do the skills that you do. Often it is this style which sets you apart from nineteen other people who can do the same tasks as you can. Therefore, *this part of the exercise should not be skipped over.* Following is a list of styles (they are often called **personal traits** or **self-management skills**; you will further note that many of them can serve as the **modifier** when you are fleshing out your skill verbs, above). Put a check mark in front of any word (or phrase) below that you think applies to you in your work. Add any others that occur to you, which are not on this list. Then when you are done checking, pick the ten that you think are **most** important, and copy them onto the bottom part of *The Tasks petal--in their order of importance to you, if you can.* This matter of *importance* will most often come down to a question of which style you are proudest of, next proudest of, and so forth. Use the Prioritizing Grid if you need to.

Style with Which I Do These Skills

I am VERY:

☐ Accurate
☐ Achievement-oriented
☐ Adaptable
☐ Adept
☐ Adept at having fun
☐ Adventuresome
☐ Alert
☐ Appreciative
☐ Assertive
☐ Astute
☐ Authoritative
☐ Calm
☐ Cautious
☐ Charismatic
☐ Competent
☐ Consistent
☐ Contagious in my enthusiasm
☐ Cooperative
☐ Courageous
☐ Creative
☐ Decisive
☐ Deliberate
☐ Dependable/have dependability
☐ Diligent
☐ Diplomatic
☐ Discreet

☐ Driving
☐ Dynamic
☐ Extremely economical
☐ Effective
☐ Energetic
☐ Enthusiastic
☐ Exceptional
☐ Exhaustive
☐ Experienced
☐ Expert
☐ Firm
☐ Flexible
☐ Humanly oriented
☐ Impulsive
☐ Independent
☐ Innovative
☐ Knowledgeable
☐ Loyal
☐ Methodical
☐ Objective
☐ Open-minded
☐ Outgoing
☐ Outstanding
☐ Patient
☐ Penetrating
☐ Perceptive
☐ Persevering
☐ Persistent

☐ Pioneering
☐ Practical
☐ Professional
☐ Protective
☐ Punctual
☐ Quick/ work quickly
☐ Rational
☐ Realistic
☐ Reliable
☐ Repeatedly
☐ Resourceful
☐ Responsible
☐ Responsive
☐ Safeguarding
☐ Self-motivated
☐ Self-reliant
☐ Sensitive
☐ Sophisticated, very sophisticated
☐ Strong
☐ Supportive
☐ Tactful
☐ Thorough
☐ Unique
☐ Unusual
☐ Versatile
☐ Vigorous

I am a person who:

With respect to execution of a task, and achievement
☐ Takes initiative
☐ Is able to handle a great variety of tasks and responsibilities simultaneously and efficiently
☐ Takes risks
☐   Takes calculated risks
☐ Is expert at getting things done

With respect to time, and achievement
☐ Consistently tackles tasks ahead of time
☐ Is adept at finding ways to speed up a task
☐ Gets the most done in the shortest time
☐ Expedites the task at hand
☐ Meets deadlines
☐   Delivers on promises on time
☐   Brings projects in on time and within budget

With respect to working conditions
☐ Maintains order and neatness in my workspace
☐ Is attendant to details
☐ Has a high tolerance of repetition and/or monotonous routines
☐ Likes planning and directing an entire activity
☐ Demonstrates mastery
☐ Promotes change
☐ Works well under pressure and still improvises
☐ Enjoys a challenge
☐ Loves working outdoors
☐ Loves to travel
☐ Has an unusually good grasp of . . .
☐ Is good at responding to emergencies
☐ Has the courage of his or her convictions

When you are done with this exercise, copy the results at the bottom of the Tasks/Skills petal.

THE EIGHTH PETAL

My Favorite
Tasks/Transferable Skills

In order to do my favorite Tasks/Skills,
I need to be using my favorite
Functional/Transferable Skills.
These are:

What I Like to Do With

THINGS	OR	PEOPLE	OR	INFORMATION/IDEAS

1.

2.

3.

4.

5.

6.

7.

8.

My Style
of Doing Them: (so-called "traits" or "self-management skills")
e.g., "quickly," "thoroughly," "painstakingly," etc.

My favorite and strongest skill is:

My second favorite and strongest skill is:

My third:

My fourth:

My fifth:

My sixth:

My seventh:

My eighth:

Conclusion:
Putting It All Together

Now that you have completed all of the petals, it is time to put them all together on one piece of paper. Why do you need to put all the petals together? Because, your ideal job is not going to be found lying about the countryside in eight separate pieces; it will be a unity, and so must your picture of it be, that you carry in your mind (or in your notebook) as you go job-hunting.

So, don't leave the filled-out picture of the petals as they presently are - - all separated from each other, lying on separate sheets in this booklet. Please cut out the circles of each petal and paste them, or photocopy them - - all of them - - onto one piece of paper.

Obviously, you will need a large sheet of blank paper on which to do this. You may make this sheet most easily by simply taping together nine sheets of plain 8½ x 11 inch paper as shown here:

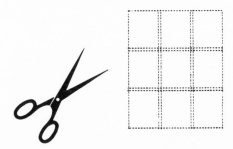

Or, if you want to avoid all this taping, you may go to any art supply or large stationery store, and buy a sheet of paper or cardboard there that is about 24 x 36 inches in size. When you have this larger paper, *please* paste (or copy) all your filled-out petals onto it, so that the overall picture resembles the Flower Picture on page 40.

That is what your Flower should look like, when you have it all pasted together. Each petal cuts down the territory for your job-search. So do fill out *all* these petals. You must, you must, you must *thus* cut down the territory that you now need to go exploring.

The Keys to Cutting Down the Territory

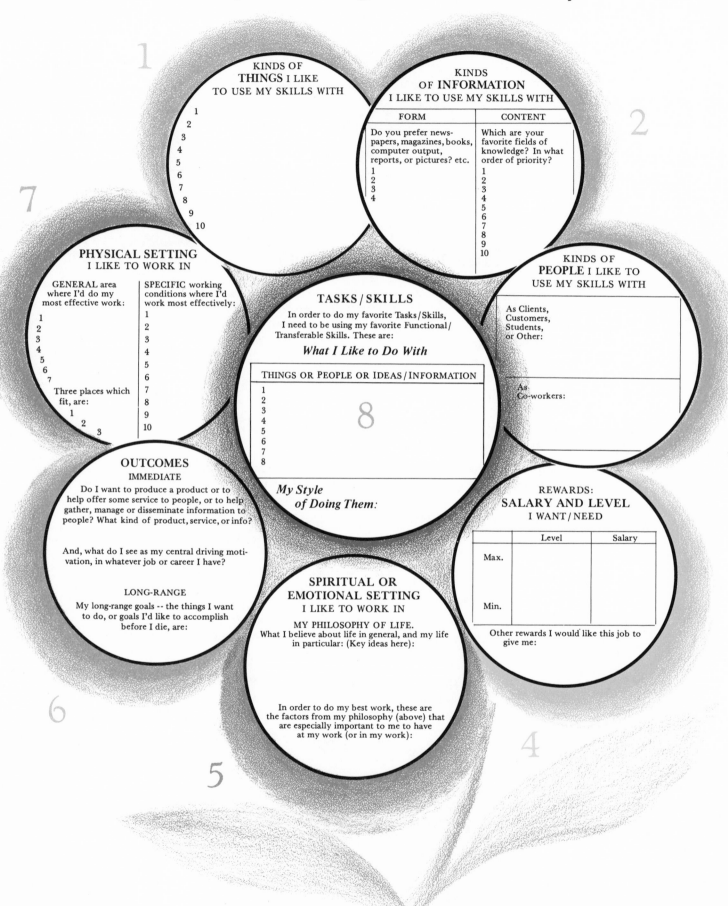

When you are satisfied with your Flower Diagram, you will then need to set out on your visits with people, for the purpose of finding out what the names are, of the jobs your flower depicts; and where those jobs are located. We call this "informational interviewing." (You may practice for it first--we call that *practice interviewing.*) In "informational interviewing," here's what you're trying to find out:

> **1** What are the names of jobs that would use my strongest and most enjoyable skills and fields of knowledge?

> **2** What kinds of organizations have such jobs?

> **3** What are the names of the organizations that I particularly like; among those uncovered in Question #2?

> **4** What needs do they have, or what outcomes are they trying to produce, that my skills could help with?

When you have found out what kinds of jobs fit your picture, then you are ready to approach places which have those kinds of jobs (also discovered during your "*informational interviewing*") and approach them for an "*employment interview.*"

The difference between these three steps is illustrated on page 42.

If you want some kind of a written career description statement to tie your Flower all together at the end of your informational interviews, here is a form you might use:

I want a post as _____ OR a challenging _____ post/position in my own organization/shop OR _____ with (a leading) _____ firm/institution/organization (seeking to _____) where/in which/requiring _____ knowledge, OR (broad) experience in _____ OR proven/demonstrated skills in _____ plus _____ can be (fully) used/utilized to (the fullest) advantage, preferably where strong background/or interest in _____ can also be additional assets.

Sample filled out form:

I want a position as a human development specialist on the staff of an educational institution that is seeking to motivate and develop students to become all that they can be through leadership, initiative and creativity, where successful experience in university administration, teaching and counseling, program development and student and public relations, plus an uncommon ability to communicate, to influence, and to persuade through public speaking, group dynamics, and high-level representational talents can be utilized to the fullest advantage.

Having Finished Your Flower,
In Order Now to Find Your Job, You Do These Three Types of Interviews In Turn

	P Pleasure	**I** Information	**E** Employment
Kind of Interview	Practice Field Survey	Informational Interviewing or Researching	Employment Interview or Hiring Interview
Purpose	To Get Used to Talking with People to Enjoy It; To "Penetrate" Networks	To Find Out If You'd Like a Job, Before You Go Trying to Get It	To Get Hired for the Work You Have Decided You Would Most Like to Do
How You Go to the Interview	You Can Take Somebody with You	By Yourself or You Can Take Somebody with You	By Yourself
Who You Talk To	Anyone Who Shares Your Enthusiasm About a (for You) Non-Job-Related Subject	A Worker Who Is Doing the Actual Work You Are Thinking About Doing	An Employer Who Has the Power to Hire You for the Job You Have Decided You Would Most Like to Do
How Long a Time You Ask For	10 Minutes (and DON'T run over -- asking to see them at 11:50 may help keep you honest, since most employers have lunch appointments at noon)		
What You Ask Them	Any Curiosity You Have About Your Shared Interest or Enthusiasm If Nothing Occurs to You, Ask: 1. How did you start, with this hobby, interest, etc.? 2. What excites or interests you the most about it? 3. What do you find is the thing you like the least about it? 4. Who else do you know of who shares this interest, hobby or enthusiasm, or could tell me more about my curiosity? a. Can I go and see them? b. May I mention that it was you who suggested I see them? c. May I say that you recommended them? *Get their name and address*	Any Questions You Have About This Job or This Kind of Work If Nothing Occurs to You, Ask: 1. How did you get interested in this work and how did you get hired? 2. What excites or interests you the most about it? 3. What do you find is the thing you like the least about it? 4. Who else do you know of who does this kind of work, or similar work but with this difference: _____? 5. What kinds of challenges or problems do you have to deal with in this job? 6. What skills do you need in order to meet those challenges or problems? *Get their name and address*	You Tell Them What It Is You Like About Their Organization and What Kind of Work You Are Looking For. You tell them the kinds of challenges you like to deal with. What skills you have to deal with those challenges. What experience you have had in dealing with those challenges in the past.
AFTERWARD: That Same Night	SEND A THANK YOU NOTE	SEND A THANK YOU NOTE	SEND A THANK YOU NOTE

© Copyright 1986 by D. Porot. Used by special permission. Not to be reproduced without permission in writing from D. Porot.

Epilogue

IF YOU HAVE COMPLETED THIS MAP, and gone about the PIE method shown on the page opposite, you will have mastered the systematic techniques that successful job-hunters and career-changers use. With a little bit of luck, these techniques should work for you as they have worked for them. "Getting lucky" is not the random chance that it would seem to be. Articles and books have been written about who "gets lucky" and who does not. If you would "get lucky," there are things you can do. Here's what we now know:

(1) **Luck favors the prepared mind.** The reason for this is not difficult to understand. If you've done all the homework on yourself, diligently identified your favorite skills, *put them in order,* and if you've gotten a pretty complete picture of the kind of job you are looking for, **you will be more sensitive and alert to luck, when it crosses your path.**

(2) **Luck favors the person who is working the hardest at the job-hunt.** In a word, the person who is devoting the most hours to getting out there and pounding the pavement, doing their research, making contacts. Luck favors the person who is putting in thirty-four hours a week on their job-hunt much more than it favors the person who is putting in five hours a week. The more you are 'out there' the more you're going to run across that fortunate coincidence that others call 'luck.'

(3) **Luck favors the person who has told the most people clearly and precisely what he or she is looking for.** The more ears and eyes you have out there, looking on your behalf for the kind of job you want, the more likely that you will 'get lucky.' Forty eyes and ears are 'luckier' than two. Eighty, a hundred and twenty, are 'luckier' still. But before you get 'this lucky,' you must have done your homework so carefully that you can tell those other eyes and ears just exactly what it is you want. Luck does not favor the vague.

(4) **Luck favors the person who has alternatives up his or her sleeve,** and doesn't just **bull-headedly** persist in following just one method, or going after just one place, or one kind of job.

(5) **Luck favors the person who WANTS WITH ALL THEIR HEART to find that job.** The ambivalent job-hunter, who is looking half-heartedly, for a job that inspires no enthusiasm in them, is rarely so 'lucky.'

(6) **Luck favors the person who is going after their dream -- the thing they really want to do the most in this world.** When you want something so much that it brings tears to your eyes at the thought of getting it, you will always be 'luckier' than the person who is settling for 'what's realistic.'

(7) **Luck favors the person who is trying hard to be 'a special kind of person' in this world, treating others with grace and dignity and courtesy and kindness.** The person who runs roughshod over others in their race to 'get ahead,' usually is not so 'lucky.' During the job-hunt you need 'favors' from others. If you treated them cavalierly in another day and age, now is their time to say, "Sure, I'll help you out," and then do nothing. **Getting even** is more popular than being helpful, if there is a score to be settled.

So, if you would have 'luck' on your side during this phase of the job-hunt, **do** take seriously the above **ways of improving your luck.**

My friend, I wish you **good luck.** I wish you **persistence.** I wish you **success,** not only with your job-hunt or career-change, but -- even more -- with your life.

Appendix

Uniquely You

A Dictionary of Skill Synonyms or Related Words

This is a supplemental section to this booklet. It is designed to be used only *after* you have identified your skills *and* chosen your favorites--your Top Ten.

You don't need to use this section at all, if you are basically satisfied with the way your skills were described on the Transferable Skills charts (pages 33-35). But most job-hunters, and career-changers in particular, *will* want to get their skills out of the standard language and into language they feel more comfortable with, because it describes their uniqueness. If you are one of those, this section is for you. **You need only look up those skills which you checked off as your favorites.**

See if anything in this section describes the skills you actually have, in a better way. You do not need to slavishly copy any phrases here. If you can think of any way to adapt them, and make them even more uniquely your own, by all means do so.

Skills with Things

If some of your favorite skills were with **Things**, those skills are listed below (in **bold** type), with the synonyms or related skills (if any) in regular type, immediately after each. Circle any that you think more accurately describe what it is you do.

I AM GOOD AT

Using my hands or fingers: good with my hands; feeling, fingering, having manual dexterity, gathering, receiving, separating, sorting, applying, pressing

Having great finger dexterity: having keen sense of touch, keyboarding, typing, playing (a musical instrument)

Using my eyes and hands in coordination: balancing, juggling, drawing, painting

Motor/physical coordination with my whole body: possessing fine motor coordination, raising, lifting, carrying, pushing, pulling, moving, unloading, walking, running, backpacking, swimming, hiking, mountaineering, skiing

Having agility, speed, strength or stamina: displaying great physical agility, possessing great strength, demonstrating outstanding endurance, maintaining uncommon physical fitness, acting as bodyguard

Crafting, sewing, weaving, hammering, etc.: knitting, collecting

Cutting, carving or chiseling: logging, mining, drawing samples from the earth

Fashioning, molding, shaping or sculpting: working (materials)

Finishing, painting, refinishing, or restoring: binding, sandblasting, grinding

Precision working with my hands: making miniatures, skilled at working in the micro-universe

Washing, cleaning or preparing:

Handling, or expediting: using particular tools (say which), placing, guiding, receiving, shipping, distributing, delivering

Making, producing, manufacturing (cooking): having great culinary skills

Maintaining, preserving, or repairing objects, tools, instruments:

Precision working with tools or instruments: precise attainment of set limits, tolerances, or standards; having great dexterity with small instruments (e.g., tweezers); keypunching; drilling; enjoy working within precise limits or standards of accuracy

Setting up or assembling: clearing, laying, installing, displaying

Operating, controlling, or driving: piloting, navigating, guiding, steering, mastering machinery against its will

Tending, minding, feeding, or emptying: monitoring machines or valves, giving continuous attention to, regulating controls of, watching to make sure nothing goes wrong, making a ready response in any emergency, checking, pushing buttons, starting, flipping switches, switching, adjusting controls, turning knobs, making adjustments when machine threatens to malfunction, placing, inserting, stacking, loading, dumping, removing, disposing of

Maintaining, cleaning or repairing equipment, machinery, or vehicles: changing, refilling, tuning, adjusting, fitting, doing preventative maintenance, trouble-shooting, restoring, fixing

Breaking down, disassembling, or salvaging: mopping up, cleaning up, knocking down

Constructing or reconstructing: erecting, putting together

Modeling or remodeling: able to perform magic on a room

Having a green thumb, causing growing things to flourish: helping to grow, farming, digging, plowing, tilling, seeding, planting, nurturing, groundskeeping, landscaping, weeding, harvesting

Having skills with animals, raising, training, or treating, etc.: animal training, ranching, sensing, persuading, etc. *With higher animals, the skills used are very similar to people skills (see below).*

Skills with People

If some of your favorite skills were with **People**, those skills are listed below (in **bold** type), with the synonyms or related skills (if any) in regular type, immediately after each. Circle any that you think more accurately describe what it is you do.

WITH INDIVIDUALS, I AM GOOD AT

Taking instructions, serving, or helping: following detailed instructions, rendering support services, preparing (something for someone), hostessing, waiting on tables, protecting, rendering services to, dealing patiently with difficult people

Communicating well in conversation, in person or on the phone: hearing and answering questions perceptively, adept at two-way dialogue, being sensitive and responsive to the feelings of others, empathizing, showing warmth, good telephoning skills, developing warmth over the telephone, creating an atmosphere of acceptance, keen ability to put self in someone else's shoes, signaling, talking, telling, informing, giving instructions, exchanging information

Communicating well in writing: (see above), also: expressing with clarity, verbalizing cogently, uncommonly warm letter composition

Instructing, teaching, tutoring, or training individuals: guiding, interpreting and expressing facts and ideas

Advising, coaching, counseling, mentoring, empowering: facilitating personal growth and development; helping people identify their problems, needs, and solutions; interpreting others' dreams; raising people's self-esteem

Diagnosing, treating, or healing: prescribing, attending, caring for, nursing, ministering to, caring for the handicapped, having true therapeutic abilities, having healing abilities, powerful in prayer, rehabilitating, curing, raising people's self-esteem

Referring people, or helping two people to link up: recommending, making and using contacts effectively, acting as a resource broker, finding people or other resources, adept at calling in other experts or helpers as needed

Assessing, evaluating, screening, or selecting individuals: having accurate gut reactions, sizing up other people perceptively, quickly assessing what's going on, realistically assessing people's needs, perceptive in identifying and assessing the potential of others, monitoring behavior through watching, critical evaluation, and feedback

Persuading, motivating, recruiting, or selling individuals: influencing, moving, inspiring, displaying charisma, inspiring trust, evoking loyalty, convincing, motivating, developing rapport or trust, recruiting talent or leadership, attracting skilled, competent and creative people, enlisting, demonstrating (a product), selling tangibles or intangibles

Representing others, interpreting others' ideas or language: translating jargon into relevant and meaningful terms, helping others to express their views, speaking a foreign language fluently, serving as an interpreter, clarifying values and goals of others, expert at liaison roles, representing a majority or minority group in a larger meeting or assembly

WITH GROUPS, I AM GOOD AT

Communicating effectively to a group or a multitude, by...

Using words expressively in speaking or writing: outstanding writing skills; making oral presentations; exceptional speaking ability; addressing large or small groups confidently; very responsive to audience's moods or ideas; thinking quickly on my feet; speechwriting, playwriting and writing with humor, fun and flair; employing humor in describing my experiences; ability to vividly describe people or scenes so that others can visualize them; very explicit and concise writing; making people think; doing excellent promotional writing; creating imaginative advertising and publicity programs, keeping superior minutes of meetings

Making presentations in person, or on TV or film: using voice tone and rhythm as unusually effective tool of communication, giving radio or TV presentations, giving briefings, making reports

Performing, entertaining, amusing, or inspiring: exhibiting showmanship, having strong theatrical sense, understudying, provoking laughter, making people laugh, distracting, diverting

Signing, miming, acting, singing, or playing an instrument: dramatizing, modeling, dancing, playing music, giving poetry readings, relating seemingly disparate ideas by means of words or actions, exceptionally good at facial expressions or body language to express thoughts or feelings eloquently

Playing games, or a particular game, leading others in recreation or exercise: excellent at sports; excellent at a particular sport (tennis, gymnastics, running, swimming, golf, baseball, football); helping others to get fit; creating, planning, and organizing outdoor activities; leading backpacking, hiking, camping, mountain-climbing expeditions; outdoor survival skills; excellent at traveling

Teaching, training, or designing educational events: lecturing; explaining; instructing; enlightening; demonstrating; showing; detailing; modeling (desired behavior); patient teaching; organizing and administering in-house training events; planning and carrying out well-run seminars, workshops, or meetings; fostering a stimulating learning environment; ability to shape the atmosphere of a place so that it is warm, pleasant, and comfortable; instilling in people a love of the subject being taught; explaining difficult or complex concepts or ideas; putting things in perspective; showing others how to take advantage of a resource; helping others to experience something; making distinctive visual presentations

Guiding a group discussion, conveying warmth: skilled at chairing meetings; group-facilitating; refusing to put people into slots or categories; treating others as equals, without regard to education, authority, or position; discussing; conferring; exchanging information; drawing out people; encouraging people; helping people make their own discoveries; helping people identify their own intelligent self-interest; adept at two-way dialogue; ability to hear and answer questions perceptively

Persuading a group, debating, motivating, or selling: publicizing, promoting, reasoning persuasively, influencing the ideas and attitudes of others, selling a program or course of action to decision-makers, obtaining agreement after the fact, fund-raising, arranging financing, writing a proposal, promoting or bringing about major policy changes, devising a systematic approach to goal setting

Consulting, giving advice to groups in my area of expertise: advising, giving expert advice or recommendations, trouble-shooting, giving professional advice, giving insight concerning

Managing, supervising, or running a business, fund drive, etc.: coordinating, overseeing, heading up, administering, directing, controlling (a project), conducting (an orchestra), directing (a production, or play), planning, organizing, and staging of theatrical productions, adept at planning and staging ceremonies, deft at directing creative talent, interpreting goals, promoting harmonious relations and efficiency, encouraging people, organizing my time expertly, setting up and maintaining on-time work schedules, establishing effective priorities among competing requirements, coordinating operations and details, sizing up situations, anticipating people's needs, deals well with the unexpected or critical event, skilled at allocating scarce financial resources, bringing projects in on time and within budget, able to make hard decisions

Following through, getting things done, producing: executing, carrying out decisions reached, implementing decisions, expediting, building customer loyalty, unusual ability to work self-directedly without supervision, able to handle a variety of tasks and responsibilities simultaneously and efficiently, instinctively gathering resources even before the need for them becomes clear, recognizing obsolescence of ideas or procedures before compelling evidence is yet at hand, anticipating problems or needs before they become problems, decisive in emergencies, continually searching for more responsibility, developing or building markets for ideas or products, completing, attaining objectives, meeting goals, producing results, delivering as promised, increasing productivity, making good use of feedback

Leading, taking the lead, being a pioneer: determining goals, objectives, and procedures, making policy, willing to experiment with new approaches, recognizing and utilizing the skills of others, organizing diverse people into a functioning group, unifying, energizing, team-building, delegating authority, sharing responsibility, taking manageable risks, instinctively understand political realities, acting on new information immediately, seek and seize opportunities

Initiating, starting up, founding, or establishing: originating, instituting, establishing, charting, financing startups

Negotiating between two parties, or resolving conflicts: mediating, arbitrating, bargaining, umpiring, adjudicating, renegotiating, reconciling, resolving, achieving compromise, charting mergers, getting diverse groups to work together, adept at conflict management, accepting of differing opinions, handling prima donnas tactfully and well, collaborating with colleagues skillfully, handling super-difficult individuals in situations, without stress, skilled at arriving at jointly agreed-upon decisions or policy or program or solutions, working well in a hostile environment, confronting others with touchy or difficult personal matters, treating people fairly.

Skills with Information

If some of your favorite skills were with **Information**, those skills are listed below (in **bold** type), with the synonyms or related skills (if any) in regular type, immediately after each. Circle any that you think more accurately describe what it is you do.

I AM GOOD AT

Compiling, searching, or researching: have exceptional intelligence tempered by common sense; like dealing with ideas, information and concepts; exhibit a perpetual curiosity and delight in new knowledge; relentlessly curious; have a love of printed things; reading avidly; reading ceaselessly; committed to continual personal growth, and learning; continually seeking to expose self to new experiences; love to stay current, particularly on the subjects of . . . ; continually gathering information with respect to a particular problem or area of expertise (say *what*); finding and getting things not easy to find; searching databases; discovering; discovering resources, ways, and means; investigating; detecting; surveying; identifying; ascertaining; determining; finding; assembling; compiling; gathering; collecting; surveying organizational needs; doing economic research

Gathering information by interviewing, or observing people: skilled at striking up conversations with strangers, talking easily with all kinds of people, adept at gathering information from people by talking to them, listening intently and accurately, intuiting, inquiring, questioning people gently, highly observant of people, learn from the example of others, study other people's behavior perceptively, accurately assessing public moods

Gathering information by studying, or observing things: paying careful attention to, being very observant, keenly aware of surroundings, examining, concentrating, focusing on minutiae

Having an acute sense of hearing, smell, taste, or sight: ability to distinguish different musical notes, perfect pitch, having uncommonly fine sense of rhythm, possessing color discrimination of a very high order, possessing instinctively excellent taste in design, arrangement, and color

Imagining, inventing, creating, or designing new ideas: devising, generating, innovating, formulating, conceptualizing, having conceptual ability of a high order, hypothesizing, discovering, conceiving new concepts, approaches, interpretations, being an idea man or woman, having "ideaphoria," demonstrating originality, continually conceiving, generating and developing innovative and creative ideas, creative imagining, possessed of great imagination, having imagination and the courage to use it, improvising on the spur of the moment, composing (music), continually conceiving, generating and developing music, continually creating new ideas for systems, methods, and procedures

Copying, and/or comparing similarities or differences: addressing, posting, making comparisons, checking, proofreading, perceiving identities or divergencies, developing a standard or model, estimating (e.g., the speed of a moving object), comparing with previous data

Computing, working with numbers, doing accounting: counting, taking inventory, counting with high accuracy, having arithmetical skills, calculating, performing rapid and accurate manipulation of numbers, in my head or on